"They're a very successful family!"

JOSEPH FARRIS

A long-time contract cartoonist with *The New Yorker,* Joseph Farris has produced a steady stream of memorable cartoons for that magazine. They have included a number on his favorite subject — the foibles and frustrations of suburban living — many of which are collected for the first time in this book along with cartoons from other publications.

Known for his incisive captions as well as the excellence of his drawing, Farris carries his talents over to the fine arts. His sculptures and abstract paintings have won awards and are in many private collections. Many of his works decorate his rambling house and studio on a high hilltop in Bethel, Connecticut, where he lives with his wife Cynthia, an art teacher and an artist in her own right.

"They're a very successful family!"

The Vagaries and Vicissitudes of
LIFE AMONG SUBURBIA'S UPSCALERS

Cartoons by JOSEPH FARRIS

Published by Spectacle Lane Press

For Cynthia

"I've called the family together to announce that, because of inflation, I'm going to have to let two of you go."

"Crocuses! It's spring!"

"I'm about to have a tantrum. What are you doing?"

"Will you marry us?"

"Relax. The important thing is that he drinks his milk, not how."

"Enough frank and honest talk. Let's go back to hypocrisy and dishonest talk."

"Just keep saying to yourself 'I'm not a sexist, I'm not a sexist . . .'"

"I listen to Peter Jennings, MacNeil/Lehrer and Elsie here."

"Enjoy the rat race, dear."

*"My parents try so hard to do the right things for me,
but, unfortunately, they're always wrong."*

LOSEPH FARRIS

"That's a tidy one."

"I love your cardiovascular system!"

"Rick and I have decided to be more sensitive."

"How sweet of you!"

"I'm feeling marvelous, Ian. No sobering thoughts, please."

"There's no such thing as 'safe sex'!"

*"I'd like a ring, but nothing too expensive.
This is only my first marriage."*

"I'm sorry, but there's nothing in the zoning regulations covering bad taste."

"Isn't that cute! They're thanking us."

"No contract, no work."

"*I **told** you this was a rough hole!*"

"We're slowly disappearing, Marty. Shouldn't we do something?"

"Gimme, gimme, gimme!"

"Isn't that nice! The Kaltons have an all-computerized house."

"Celeste is into plants and I'm into books."

"I don't want to see, smell, feel or taste a zucchini ever again!"

*"It started out as a little tree house for the kids
and we kept adding on to it."*

"George! Come and look at your squirrel-proof feeder!"

"It was a great party. Now I know what 'the opposite sex' means!"

"There isn't a damn thing worth watching anywhere in the world."

"I love our hideaway. I only wish we could find it!"

"You INGRATE! DESERTER! SELFISH MAN! I dreamed you won $24 million in the lottery and you promptly left me!"

"Don't you think we've already been to one crafts fair too many?"

"Look who's up for the weekend again."

*"Mommy loves you but Mommy has to move out.
Daddy will feed you, wash your clothes, clean the house,
do the shopping, take you to the doctor . . ."*

*"Do you suppose nobody pays any attention to us because
we've only been married once?"*

"You'll be happy to know, Father, he's not a Liberal,
Moderate or Conservative. Jason's a nothing."

"For Roger it's the realization of a lifelong quest — the perfect lawn."

"Do you ever get the feeling that baseball is a national obsession?"

"You're not living up to your potential!"

"Harry, she just said her first words! She said, 'Why have you saddled my generation with the huge national debt?'"

"Listen to me, all of you. There's a big economic crunch out there so we're all going to have to tighten our belts and eat less."

*"Goodbye, dear. This is the kind of a day
that makes you feel glad to be alive!"*

"This is a helluva time to tell me you don't like this location."

"Every time I pass through here I get heartburn."

*"I know **who** I am but I don't know **what** I am!"*

"Rodman has a marvelous green thumb. He can grow things anywhere!"

"Let's face it. We have an environmental crisis of our own!"

" . . . And a free set of tools goes with it."

*"It didn't work out. He liked Northern Italian cooking
and I liked Southern Italian cooking."*

Joseph
Farris

"What'll I do with the nuclear wastes?"

"May I have a moment of your time? I'd like to tell you about a plan my bank has for your IRA . . ."

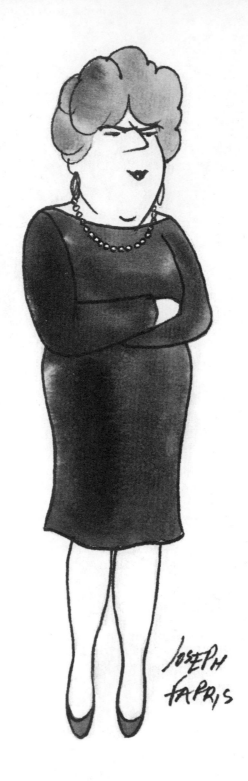

Built to Last.

"They're a very successful family."

"Are you here, Alfred?"

JOSEPH
FARRIS

Mythical Family of Four

"I have kindergarten burnout!"

*"I'm going to watch the news. Do you know
where my rose-colored glasses are?"*

"We only live once. Hop in."

"Bad news! More and more people are switching from red meat to fish!"

"How much did you say we'd be saving by buying a wood-burning stove?"

"*I'm your new daughter. Marcia and I have traded parents.*"

"Good Lord! Their basic house wine is the same as ours."

"Maybe it's one of those super-stations."

"Frankly, we're just keeping our heads above water."

"There's nothing good to eat!"

Simulated Picture

"We got tired of being broken into!"

"It's my main decorating motif."

"Come quick — a pileated woodpecker!"

"This country has been good to me."

"Hold on, Baby, hold on!"

NO! NO! NO! NO! NO! NO!
NO! NO! NO! NO! NO!
NO! NO! NO! NO! NO! NO! NO! NO! NO!
NO! NO! NO! NO! NO! NO NO! NO!
NO! NO! NO! NO! NO NO! NO! NO!
NO! NO! NO!
NO! NO! NO! NO NO! NO! NO!
NO! NO! NO! NO! NO! NO!
NO! NO! NO! NO!
NO! NO! NO! NO!
NO! NO! NO! NO! NO!
NO! NO! NO! NO!
NO! NO! NO! NO! NO!
NO! NO! NO! NO! NO!
NO! NO! NO! NO! NO!
NO! NO! NO! NO! NO!
NO! NO! NO! NO! NO! NO! NO!
NO! NO! NO! NO! NO! NO!
NO! NO! NO! NO! NO! NO! NO!
NO! NO! NO! NO! NO!
NO! NO! NO! NO! NO! NO! NO! NO!
JOSEPH FARRIS

Published by Spectacle Lane Press